MATH EVERY DAY

Animals Big and Small

Daniel Nunn

Raintree
Chicago, Illinois

www.capstonepub.com
Visit our website to find out more information about Heinemann-Raintree books.

To order:
Phone 800-747-4992
Visit www.capstonepub.com to browse our catalog and order online.

© 2012 Raintree
an imprint of Capstone Global Library, LLC
Chicago, Illinois

All rights reserved. No part of this publication may be reproduced or transmitted in any form or by any means, electronic or mechanical, including photocopying, recording, taping, or any information storage and retrieval system, without permission in writing from the publisher.

Edited by Daniel Nunn, Rebecca Rissman, and Sian Smith
Designed by Joanna Hinton-Malivoire
Picture research by Elizabeth Alexander
Illustrations by Joanna Hinton-Malivoire
Originated by Capstone Global Library Ltd.
Production by Victoria Fitzgerald

Library of Congress Cataloging-in-Publication Data
Nunn, Daniel.
Animals big and small / Daniel Nunn.
p. cm. – (Math every day)
Includes bibliographical references and index.
ISBN 978-1-4329-5733-9 (hb) – ISBN 978-1-4329-5738-4 (pb)
1. Size perception–Juvenile literature. 2. Body size–Juvenile literature. 3. Comparison (Philosophy)–Juvenile literature. I. Title.
BF299.S5N86 2012
153.7'52–dc23
2011013021

Acknowledgments
We would like to thank the following for permission to reproduce photographs: iStockphoto p. 14 (© Christian Weibell); Shutterstock pp. 4–5 (© Eric Isselée), 6 left (© Lisa A. Svara), 6 right (© photobac), 7 (© Eric Isselée), 8, 9 right (© joyfull), 9 left (© Gelpi), 10 left (© Christian Musat), 10 right, 11 (© Kletr), 12 right (© Eric Isselée), 12 left (© Sergii Figurnyi), 13 top (© Alexander Ishchenko), 13 bottom (© Eric Isselée), 15 (© Andre Goncalves), 16 (© Galushko Sergey), 17 (© Krzysztof Odziomek), 18 left (© Verena Lüdemann), 18 right (© Michael C. Gray), 19 (© Pichugin Dmitry), 20 (© FloridaStock), 21 (© kurdistan), 22–23 (© Susan Schmitz)

Cover photograph of a chihuahua on the back of a Great Dane reproduced with permission of Getty Images (Brand X Pictures). Back cover photograph of a cat reproduced with permission of Shutterstock (© Eric Isselée); photograph of a mouse Shutterstock (© Sergii Figurnyi).

Every effort has been made to contact copyright holders of any material reproduced in this book. Any omissions will be rectified in subsequent printings if notice is given to the publisher.

Printed in the United States 5657

Contents

Animal Sizes 4
Big and Small 6
Tall and Short 10
Long and Short 14
Wide and Narrow 18
The Same Size 22
Index 24

Animal Sizes

Let's look at animals.
They are all different sizes.

Whether big, small, or tiny
they are full of surprises!

Big and Small

Dog 1 is **big**.

Dog 2 is **small**.

Dog 3 is the **biggest** dog of them all.

Here are two horses, lined up in a row.

Is Holly bigger than Heather? Let's see if you know!

Tall and Short

Here are two more animals.
Which one is tall?

If you said the giraffe,
you made a good call!

What about these two?

Which one is shorter,
which one is taller?

Well, the cat is the tall one!
The mouse is much smaller!

Long and Short

This snake is long.
It's a bit of a whopper.

This insect is short.
It's a tiny grasshopper.

Under the water, a short orange fish swims by.

A long grey fish swims closer,
it looks like it's saying "Hi!"

Wide and Narrow

This antelope is narrow.

This hippo is **wide**.

You wouldn't have much luck getting a hippo to hide.

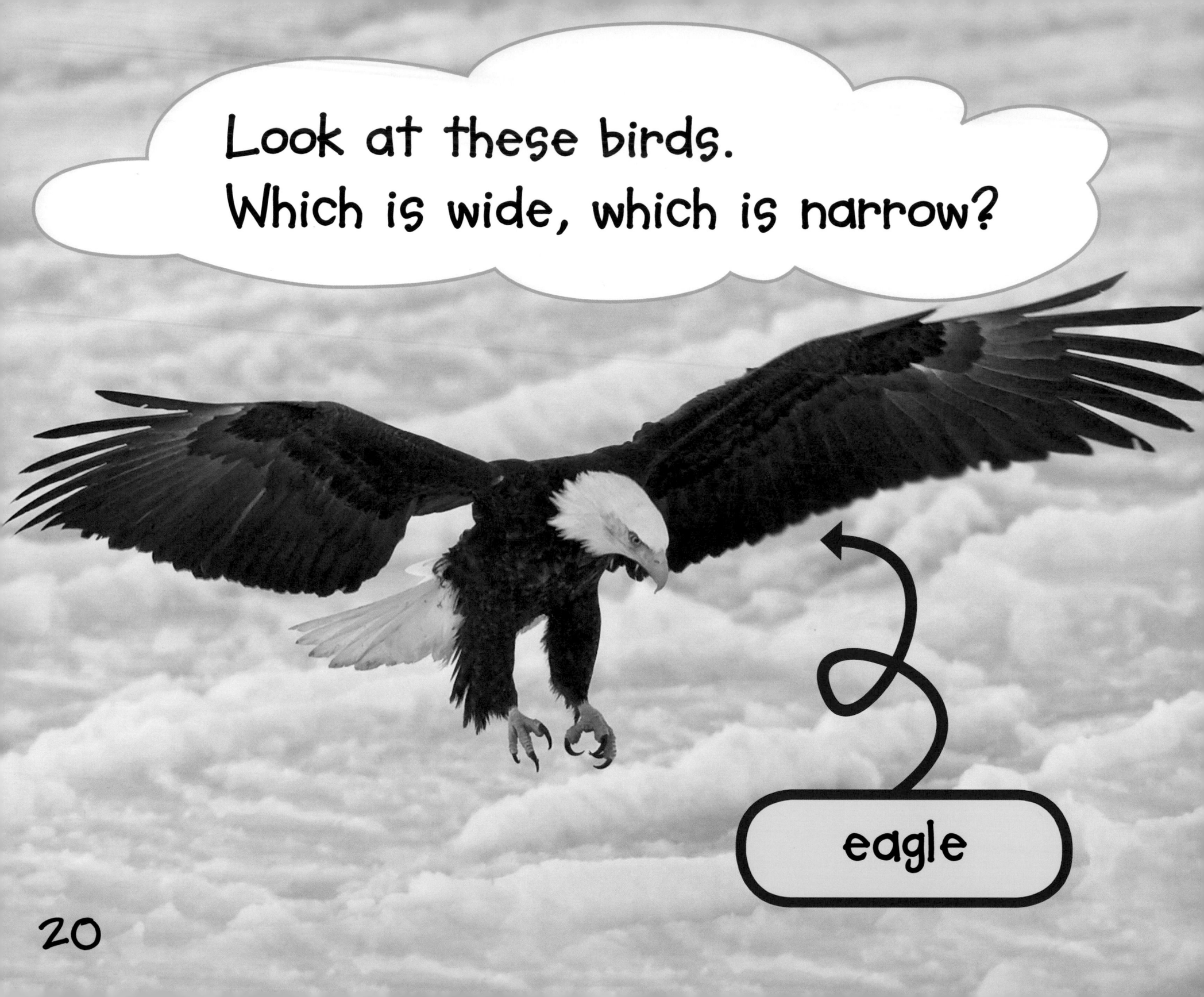
Look at these birds.
Which is wide, which is narrow?
eagle

It's easy! The eagle is wider than that tiny sparrow.

The Same Size

Which dog is the biggest, or are they all the same size?

You could use a ruler,
or just use your eyes.

Answer on page 24

Index

birds 20, 21
cats 12, 13
dogs 6, 7, 22, 23
farm animals 4, 5
fish 16, 17
horses 5, 8, 9
insects 15
mice 12, 13
quiz 22, 23
zoo animals 10, 11, 14, 18, 19

Answer to question on page 22

The dogs are all different sizes. The first dog is the biggest dog. It is bigger than all the others.